THE NEW GOLD STOCK

INVESTING ESSENTIALS

Supercharge Your Portfolio With Precious
Metals And Our Top Mining Stocks

MICHAEL SWANSON

by Michael Swanson
© 2014

ISBN: 150060092X
ISBN-13: 9781500600921

"People usually think that progress consists in the increase of knowledge, in the improvement of life, but that isn't so. Progress consists only in the greater clarification of answers to the basic questions of life. The truth is always accessible to a man. It can't be otherwise, because a man's soul is a divine spark, the truth itself. It's only a matter of removing from this divine spark (the truth) everything that obscures it. Progress consists, not in the increase of truth, but in freeing it from its wrappings. The truth is obtained like gold, not by letting it grow bigger, but by washing off from it everything that isn't gold." - Leo Tolstoy

CONTENTS

INTRODUCTION vii
THE POWER OF GOLD

CHAPTER I I
THE NEW GOLD BULL MARKET

CHAPTER II 23
THE FUNDAMENTAL FACTORS BEHIND GOLD

CHAPTER III 45
HOW TO PROFIT FROM THIS GOLD BULL MARKET
THE GOLD INDUSTRY
TYPES OF GOLD STOCKS
CHOOSING GOLD COMPANIES AS INVESTMENTS
HOW MINING COMPANIES ARE DEVELOPED

CHAPTER IV 60
SOME OF MY TOP STOCK PICKS
PICK NUMBER ONE: PERSEUS MINING (TSX: PRU)

PICK NUMBER TWO: FREEPORT-MCMORAN COPPER AND GOLD (NYSE: FCX)
PICK NUMBER THREE: ATICO MINING (VANCOUVER: ATY)

ACKNOWLEDGEMENTS 71

ABOUT THE AUTHOR...................73

INTRODUCTION
THE POWER OF GOLD

This book contains invaluable information for you. I have been investing in the financial markets now for over fifteen years and have been writing and talking to people about them since 1999. If you have been in the markets for at least as long as I have than you have seen many wild bubbles and busts. You have seen giant trends and opportunities too, but very few people have really taken advantage of them. In fact, I think it's easy to say that for most people the financial markets have been a stressful and confusing thing for them to be a part of.

You saw the rise of the internet stock bubble in 1999 and the subsequent tech wreck. You heard stories of people flipping homes in 2005 and then witnessed a crash in real estate prices that caused many to lose their homes. Maybe the real estate bust hurt you. The biggest banks on Wall Street went under in 2008 and the Federal government bailed them out to the tune of over a trillion dollars.

Yes it is true that even if the average man in the street got caught holding the bag some people did make money from the internet stock bubble and from the mortgage boom too. Some even understood what was going to happen and knew to get in the party and then get out before it came to an end. Investing can feel like playing a risky game of musical chairs. It can seem like the average individual investor is always a few steps behind; always moving too slow and acting when it is too late. So he gets trapped buying into big bull market tops and sells out on bottoms, over and over again.

The problem is that most people simply do not understand how financial markets work so they do not know when they should be buying and when they should be selling. They do not know how to get into a new big trend early before it really goes up. So they follow the always too late crowd. All most people do is turn on their TV to CNBC or some other financial channel and listen to some expert and do what they are told. But, Wall Street does not care about them.

Imagine if you bought stock in Amazon.com, Apple, or eBay way back in 1995 and sold out at the market top in March of 2000 before they collapsed for a few years. You would have made a killing if you had done that. Imagine if you knew to bet against the stock market in the summer of 2008 before it crashed that Fall. If you had done that too you would have made a lot of money while just about everyone else lost. Some people did just that.

Yes, I know that those opportunities are all in the past. It is too late to go back and do any of that. They say hindsight is 20/20 and it is. You cannot live in the past. You cannot beat yourself up over lost opportunities. You just did not know and no one can know everything. Nor can you get in on everything. All you need to know now is what the next big opportunity is going to be.

I believe gold is that opportunity. In fact, I am so convinced of this fact that I have put a substantial amount of my own money into investing in gold, silver, and into the shares of mining stocks that mine them out of the ground. I believe that they are starting a new bull market that will last for several years to the benefit of those with the foresight to purchase gold and silver now and to invest in the right mining stocks. And I felt like I had to write this book to inform you about what I believe is coming in order to help you.

You see, I believe gold represents the best chance for you to get in early on the next big trend. This is the power of gold. But I also believe that it can mean more for you than simply increasing your wealth or making some extra money. I believe that the true power of gold may actually mean something even more important to your investment life.

In the long-run, the most successful investors understand market trends and how to adapt to them. If you participate in the gold market over the next few years and learn from your experiences in it you will become a better and wiser investor. By learning how big trends impact gold you will be able to identify the start of other big bull markets and buying opportunities elsewhere too.

So gold does not represent just a new thing for you to make money in, but something that will enable you to learn how financial markets operate so that you will finally be able to take control of your investments and thrive. If you win at gold, not from just dumb luck, but from knowledge, than you will have the confidence to do so elsewhere too. That is what this book is really about and why I believe you will find it so invaluable.

Winning at the game of investing is about knowing how to recognize and seize opportunities when they come. And they do not come every day. But instead of waiting for something good most people just throw their money at the stock market and hope it will go up forever for them. You need to be patient and invest when you see something that provides the giant risk to reward chances that are truly worth betting on. It takes understanding this to become an investment superman.

Probably the most famous investor in America is Warren Buffett. People have learned a lot from his wit and wisdom. One of the parables he likes to tell is to think about the decisions you will make as an investor as a twenty-hole punch card. "I could improve your ultimate financial welfare," he said, "by giving you a ticket with only twenty slots in it so that you had twenty punches - representing all the investments that you got to make in a lifetime. And once you'd punched through the card, you couldn't make any more investments at all. Under those rules, you'd really think carefully about what you did, and you'd be forced to load up on what you'd really thought about. So you'd do so much better."

People feel like they have to be doing something all of the time when it comes to their investing, but the reality is that you only need to get in early on a few great investments to build a lot of wealth through your investing lifetime. What you should do is do everything possible to uncover those big opportunities to risk a little and make a lot. Only then should you bet big.

What you need to do is learn to understand market trends so that you'll be able to spot new big trends that will last for years just as they start. Many of the greatest investors of our generation are betting now on silver and gold.

Hedge fund manager John Paulson, who made billions by having the foresight to use credit default swaps to bet against subprime mortgages before the crash of 2008, has invested billions of dollars in gold ever since with several hedge funds that he setup just for that purpose. David Einhorn, who setup a hedge fund in 1996 with $900,000 in investment money and went on to become a billionaire thanks to the 20% annualized returns he generated in his fund, has also become a giant gold investor. For fun he also bought a minority stake in the New York Mets. As of the end of 2013, he had purchased over seven million shares of gold stock ETF GDX.

George Soros has also built up a massive position in gold mining stocks. As of the first quarter of 2014, his family office owns over six million shares of Barrick Gold and call options that give him the ability to buy two million more. He also owns over two million shares of Cameco, which is the largest uranium mining company in the world, and he has close to a million shares of the gold stock ETF GDX and a half a million shares of the junior mining ETF GDXJ.

You may not like George Soros, because of his role in politics. He is a big demon on FOX News and Bill O'Reilly and Rush Limbaugh attack him constantly for his funding of liberal causes, but like him or hate him, he is one of the most successful investors of the past fifty years and he knows how to make money. If gold goes up in the next few years he will make another fortune. Of course, his former business partner, Jim Rogers, has been hot on commodities, silver, and gold for several years now too.

In the past few years, large institutional investors have also been accumulating gold. Under the guidance of hedge fund king Kyle Bass, the University of Texas bought over a billion dollars worth of gold bars in 2011 for its endowment fund, which is the second largest in the country behind Harvard's. The University of Texas placed over 664,300 ounces of gold bullion inside a Comex vault in New York City.

Nations with trade surpluses whose central banks are generating extra dollars have also been converting some of those dollars into gold. According to data from the International Monetary Fund, China's central bank has over 1,000 tonnes of gold in its vaults. So do the central banks of Germany and Russia. The IMF itself has over 2,100 tonnes in its own reserves.

Yes, I have physical gold stashed away somewhere and I think you should own gold too. Before you read any further though I must tell you for full disclosure and regulatory purposes that you can lose money if you buy gold, or any other precious metals, and by investing in the financial markets. Nothing is guaranteed to go up for you after you buy it. Markets go up and down. If you buy on margin and things go against you then you can totally wipe yourself out. You must be prudent to be safe.

This book contains several individual stock ideas that I believe can do great for you, but I am not a registered investment advisor. It may be best for you to consult with a registered adviser or broker in order to get their opinion on any investment you are considering, including gold.

I have to tell you, though, that Wall Street as a whole hates gold and most people who work for brokerage houses also hate it. Most investment advisers and stock brokers make money by getting clients to invest in mutual funds and other products their firms create for investors. Typically, a money manager will make a commission trail for investing their client's money into a fund. They stand to make nothing though if a client takes their money out of their hands and uses it to buy physical gold or silver. As a result, most Wall

Street machines simply treat gold as a "barbaric" metal to avoid at all costs.

When dealing with any investment adviser it is always best to ask them what they are actually doing with their money. Are they personally investing in the funds they recommend to their clients? Do they understand the power of gold? If they have not been able to make themselves rich and wealthy in the financial markets than is it realistic to think that they have the ability to do that for you? These are all things to consider when dealing with anyone who works for one of the brokerage houses. Investing can be a lonely place for someone looking for a person who can really help them.

Who am I? If you do not know already, I run a financial website called WallStreetWindow.com and operate a small private group on it. If you want to know more about me and find out what I have to say going forward then you should go to that website.

From 2003 to 2006 I ran a hedge fund that generated a return of over 78% during that time frame and in one year was ranked in the top thirty-five funds out of over five-thousand tracked by performance by hedgefund.net. I'm not perfect, though. In the first year of the fund's existence I barely made anything even though the stock market went up a lot. I made a killing in the 2008 market crash personally betting against stocks but didn't adjust to the new bull market in 2009 until a few months after the bottom. I started buying gold stocks though in 2002 when gold was under $300 an ounce. Even though I have been in and out of the gold market several times since then, I now believe gold is going to go up for several years. Therefore, it is no longer to trade in and out of gold, but to buy and hold for the duration.

Let me show you why.

CHAPTER I
THE NEW GOLD BULL MARKET

Yes, I believe gold is in a new bull market that will make fortunes for people who buy it and invest in the best gold mining stocks. Before you accept that statement though you must understand what I mean by a bull market. You need to know what a bull market really is. Most people approach their investment decisions with muddled thinking. They simply have no idea of what they are doing, because they have no concept of what is happening in the financial markets. As a result their financial lives simply rise and fall with big market moves. They are like a boat with no direction in the sea. What you need is total clarity of thinking.

Let me explain what I mean so that you can understand what I mean by a bull market, because clear concepts lead to clear thinking. Now most people think a bull market is simply when prices go up. If they buy a stock or own an investment, like a mutual fund, and it goes up they are happy. To them that is a bull market. There is some truth to that, but you need to know more in order to make wise decisions.

The average person usually gets involved in a bull market when they hear other people tell them that there is a bull market to make money in or when others show them that they are making money in it. Unfortunately, this means that they usually end up getting into the market after it already has gone up for years on end and after most people they know have already gotten in. As a result, most people get stuck in market tops.

To the mass man investing is simply following the crowd and buying when things are going up and people tell them to buy. Most people look up to experts on financial television and trust them to tell them when to buy. If they get into the stock market, they'll turn on the TV and hear people tell them it's a bull market and prices are going to keep going up. They hear only what they want to hear and listen to those that give them the confirmation their brain craves as proof that they are making a wise decision. But all they are doing is following the crowd.

The most successful investors in the world do not simply chase markets and stocks after they go up. They understand what they are buying. Stocks represent ownership in a company. Stocks have a fundamental valuation based on the value of the earnings a company generates and the overall assets it owns. Stock investors who look to buy cheap stocks look at such metrics as book value, earnings growth, PEG ratios, and dividends. If the price is right for them they buy and they often will sell when they believe a stock price has reached a high valuation.

That is what real investing is about. And you can look at the overall valuation of a market to see if a market as a whole is a good investment or not from the angle of fundamental valuation. No bull market goes on forever and after a bull market ends a bear market strikes that wipes out millions of investors who refused to sell when the getting was good. They had no idea what they were doing. They simply chased the market up when it was too late. Those that buy in at the top get caught holding the bag.

Investing is not buying something because it has a hot story or simply because of earnings growth. Real investing means buying something at a good valuation. You want to make money by bargain buying at the right time. Imagine if someone came up to you with an opportunity to buy a popular restaurant in the town you live in. It's a place you go to yourself a lot and all of your friends do too. The family that owns this restaurant decides they want to retire. They offer to sell it to you for three million dollars.

Let us say you talk to your wife about it. She loves the idea. You tell some of your friends and they think it will be cool for you too. You realize that if you buy this restaurant you will become a big shot in town, because everyone who is important eats there. The steaks there are good and the drinks are fun.

So you go to your local bank and get a loan for three million dollars. You go buy the restaurant and go for it. People pat you on the back. They come to see you and the place is busy. But after a month you realize something is wrong. You look at your sales and see that you spent more money than you made in the last thirty days. The restaurant only made $15,000 and your expenses were close to $30,000. You had to pay the bank just $15,000 alone and you had expenses for food and labor. You not only have a big mess on your hands, but a disaster.

In a year you realize you are not going to be able to make it. You fall behind in your bank payments. You go bankrupt and wipe yourself out. Your friends don't understand what happened. The restaurant is great. People think that maybe something is just wrong with you. You are embarrassed. What went wrong?

The problem is that you paid a sky high stupid price for the restaurant. The restaurant made essentially $150,000 a year and you paid twenty times revenue for it. You paid such a high price that you couldn't even service your debt. Smart business people look to pay less than six times earnings for a stable business, but you did not care what price you paid. You didn't even consider it. It was a neat idea not thought through. The result was muddled thinking that lead to practical stupidity.

This is the type of foolish way that most people treat investing in stocks and the stock market as a whole. Most people pay zero attention to the price they pay to get into a stock. All they do is buy something, because they have seen it go up and therefore assume it will go up more or because someone told them a good story. Maybe they heard an analyst on TV say the stock has good earnings growth or the company it represents is coming out with a hot product. People buy into neat ideas that turn into stock disasters.

What happens is that people tend to end up behind the curve over and over again. They don't pay any attention to market trends in any meaningful way. Now people do experience the stock market in an emotional manner. They see it go up or down over time and generally speaking become influenced by whatever has taken place in the previous six to twelve months. So if a market has gone down for six months they get really bearish and sell out and if it has gone up for longer than six months they get bullish and excited, no matter what. And in fact, the longer something goes up the more bullish the masses get. High prices drive people into the stock market.

Most people look at a financial market and get scared or confused when they look at the day-to-day up and down moves. They want to know what is going on so their brain tries to make order out of the chaos. As a result, their brain becomes brainwashed by the market action of the past six months. It then assumes whatever trend has been in place during that time will essentially last forever. Their brain then interprets all news and market action as evidence that this assumption is correct. What this means is that for most people a bull market is simply a market that has gone up long enough to convince them that it will keep going up and a bear market is a market that has fallen for a long enough time to make them want to sell.

The result of this is muddled thinking that causes some-one to sell out near bear market bottoms and get trapped in tops over and over again. People miss the important turning points in the markets that make for the true great invest-ment buy points and times to sell. The problem is that most people in the end do not make much money in the market and many lose a lot of money in times of trouble.

Yet, few people try to do better. To do so would require that they take the time to learn about financial trends and investing. It means reading a book like this or taking courses. And the masses are too lazy for that. They'd rather just turn on the TV, buy into hot stories, and follow the crowd. So, they get the results of the crowd.

The best time to invest into a stock market or any finan-cial asset class, such as metals and mining stocks, is after a bear market. After a bear market stocks in a sector are cheap and make great investments, because they have tremendous upside potential from a fundamental standpoint. Most bull markets last three to five years in duration so the people who get into a bull market early make the most money while those that get in late in the game take on the most risk.

Once you understand how to really recognize a new bull market and what one really is you'll be able to get into them early. All you need to know is a few simple chart patterns and the psychological dynamics that drive markets. Even though these things are simple to understand most people simply do not want to learn them, because learning and reading a book like this takes too much work for them.

So, let us dig in together. What you need to know is that all financial markets move in bull and bear cycles that typically last three to five years. These are also in between periods between their bull and bear cycles. That makes for four cycles that you need to be aware of and to be able to recognize in order to understand the big picture of what is happening in any financial market with total clarity.

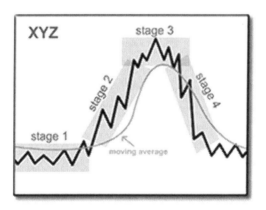

I call these cycles the four stages of a financial market. A stage one market comes after a bear market decline. It is characterized mainly by sideways price activity. It can last a few weeks and often goes on for months. Sometimes it can even go on for over a year. During a stage one market most people are actually negative about the market, because they have been brainwashed by the bear market that came before to be scared of the market. If they owned positions during the preceding bear market they suffered so much pain that they simply do not want to feel anymore. Most people who managed to hold on in the last bear market end up selling during the stage one sideways basing market.

Stocks in a stage one market are often at a super low valuation that does attract the few real fundamental investors that do exist in the market. These are the people who really know what they are doing. They buy, because things are cheap and they are willing to hold and wait for the market to recognize what they know even if it takes time. Industry insiders often buy during a stage one base, because they are able to recognize that some sort of bottom is going on in their industry. If you look at insider buying and selling data you often will find that it is during a stage one basing phase that most insider purchases take place.

However, stocks and markets in a stage one base tend to go nowhere but sideways. When they go up they have rallies that don't last and when they go down they tend to just fall and bounce back up. The temporary pullbacks, though, scare people into selling for fear of another bear market. Stage one bases fool the masses.

The reason why stocks and markets in a stage one base go sideways so much is that in the end what drives financial markets are the forces of supply and demand and nothing else. Bull markets are not created because of good news. In fact there are times when the news is good and markets fall anyway.

And, there are times when the news is bad that make for great investment buy points. Most people do nothing, though, but pay attention to the news in order to understand the reasons why a market moves even though the news is totally useless when it comes to understanding the big picture and changes in stock market cycles. What you need to understand is what really moves prices. Markets move in price trends created by the forces of supply and demand. Things are as simple as that.

Bull markets go up when there are more buyers than sellers in a market and bear markets go down when there are more sellers than buyers. In a stage one base the forces of buying and selling are actually roughly equal, which is why prices go sideways. This is what creates a stage one base.

A stage one base comes to an end when the number of buyers in a market overtakes the number of sellers. Typically, you can look at a stock chart in a stage one base and identify a resistance level that has acted as a lid on prices for some time. It is a level that has attracted sellers again and again, and has stopped rallies. When the stage one base ends this level gets smashed as the sellers liquidate their final shares. Then a new bull market begins.

The best time to invest in a market is at the end of a stage one base. The next best time is in the first few months of a new bull market. During a new bull market the buyers are in control and are able to keep bidding a market up. There are pullbacks during a bull market as some sell into rallies and many trade in and out, but such pullbacks make for great buying opportunities. Most of the gains in a stage two market actually come in the first year of a bull market. That makes getting in early really important.

As a bull market continues after the first year, more and more people get excited about the market and get in. But in the end, there is a limit to how many people and how much money there is out there to get into a market. Once that limit is reached a market will enter a stage three topping phase. Then it will begin to go sideways and many of the stocks inside the market lose momentum and turn down. Money goes into fewer and fewer stocks. However, most people are incredibly bullish during a topping market, because their brains have been programmed by the bull market moves of the past to believe the market is going to go up forever.

Stocks get expensive in a stage three topping market, but the masses don't care. Insiders sell out to take advantage of the high valuations that the masses are now willing to pay to get in stocks. All the masses care about is that stocks have gone up and may go up more. They become willing to pay any price to get in due to their greed for more gains or simple fear of missing out while someone else could possibly make money without them.

When the masses complete their buying there is literally no longer enough buyers in the market to keep it going up. Then the sellers take over and send the market into a new bear market. As the market rolls over, the masses fail to realize what is going on, because they have been so brainwashed by the last bull market to see every dip as a buying opportunity. They were in the bull market, but they no longer are. Now rallies represent traps. The dumb money gets eaten alive by bear attacks.

The longer a bear market goes on the more pain people feel in it. The growing pain makes more and more people sell. Once someone sells, they become bearish on a market. As a bear market ends there is often a selling climax of panic as people dump their remaining stocks at once in fear and disgust. After a bear market, people who managed to hold

on continue to sell in the stage one basing phase in disap-
pointment, impatience, and simple fear whenever a pullback
in the sideways base occurs.

These cycles repeat again and again and will never go
away. They have existed throughout financial history and
are created by human nature. If you can understand these
cycles, recognize them, and act on that knowledge, you can
make money in the financial markets by buying and selling at
the best times possible and while avoiding the bear markets
that hurt so many. You will then separate yourself from the
masses and become a super investor.

It's all about making your investing decisions based on
principles grounded in the reality of the iron laws of human
nature instead of the delusions of the crowd. The good news
is that it is easy to recognize these cycles if you use some
basic technical indicators that you can find in any stock market charting program or website. They are the long-term
200 and 150-day moving averages.

A moving average is calculated by adding up all of the
price points in a given time period and dividing that time
period by the number of days in it. So a 200-day moving
average is the average price of a stock or market in the past
200 days. The 150-day moving average is the average price
over the past 150 days, and so on.

The 200-day and 150-day moving averages, when plotted
out on a chart, give you a simple way to recognize the overall
price trend you are looking at. During a bull market these moving averages go up and tend to actually act as a support level
buy point during the occasional dips and corrections that occur
from time to time in a bull market. At the same time, during a
bear market they curl down on the chart and move down and
act as resistance areas that cap rallies in bear markets.

After a bear market, these moving averages go sideways in a stage one base. This means that you can easily recognize what stage a market is in by looking at these moving averages. It also means that you can tell when a market is in a stage one base after a bear market, which makes for a great time to make some long-term investments. Investing at the start of a bull market is great as well, and being cautious after a bull market has gone on for a long-time or is actually in a bear market is prudent too. When you make investment decisions in alignment with these big trends you master the market. This is your key to the kingdom.

I talk about this concept in great detail in my previous book, *Strategic Stock Trading*, but take a look at the S&P 500 for the past twenty years to see how this plays out for yourself.

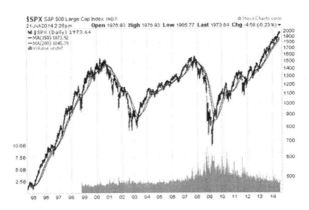

There was a little recession in the American economy during the Presidency of George H.W. Bush that caused a little bear market for the United States (US) stock market in the early 1990's and then a subsequent stage one basing phase that caused a lot of people to get out of the stock market. Once that stage one sideways basing phase ended in 1995, the S&P 500 began a giant stage two bull market that came to an end in 2000. It then went through a stage three topping market that came to an end in the fall of that year

After that the S&P 500 began a vicious stage four bear market that took prices to a bottom in 2002. Then the US stock market went through a stage one sideways basing phase that ended in 2003. A new bull market then began that lasted until 2007. Next, a short-lived stage three topping phase occurred once again that marked a transition period into a new bear market and the financial crash of 2008.

Now if you go back and look carefully at the chart of the S&P 500 you just saw you will notice that I have placed the 150 and 200-day moving averages on it. If you study this carefully you'll see what they did during all of these different market stages. As you discover the pattern you will see how clearly they act during a stage two bull market and a stage four bear market.

Look carefully and you will see that in a bull market these moving averages point up and rise. They also tend to act as support buy points for the occasional corrections that occur during a bull market. As a bull market comes to an end these moving averages tend to stop going up and spend a few months going sideways during a stage three topping phase.

During bear markets, these moving averages slope down and move down. In bear markets, the sellers are in control and send the market lower. The stock market makes lower lows and lower highs in a bear market. Rallies that are counter to the bear trend tend to come to an end at the long-term 150 and 200-day moving averages. So these averages act as tough resistance during stage four bear markets. If you held in the bear market of 2008 or after the 2000 top you probably would have done better for yourself if you had known all of this back then.

As a bear market comes to an end, though, the rate of decline in the moving averages tends to slow down. Once a bear market ends you get a stage one basing phase that acts as a transition period into a new bull market. During a stage one basing phase the moving averages bottom out and go sideways. Stage one basing phases can last a few months or even a year in duration. If you go and take the time to look at other markets you will see the same patterns repeat again and again.

Now, if we apply stage analysis to gold right now we will discover something with huge implications. Take a look at this chart of gold very closely.

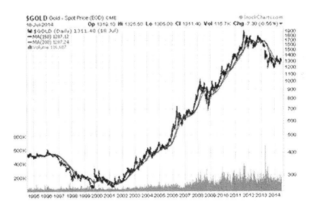

You can see that gold had a bear market from 1996 until 1999 that took it below $300 an ounce. It then went through a long stage one basing phase until 2002. After that it began a giant bull market. There was a bit of a correction in 2006 and in 2008, but gold prices skyrocketed from 2002 until they last peaked above 1,900 an ounce in 2011. You can see how during the bull market in gold how the long-term 150 and 200-day moving averages sloped up and acted as support buy points.

Now after gold topped out in 2011, it went into a stage three topping phase that ended in 2013 and brought a big bear drop that year. Gold prices went into a stage one base after bottoming in the spring of 2013. You can see how the moving averages are now going sideways, which tells us that a stage one base is occurring for gold prices.

Gold currently has resistance at 1,400 and support at 1,200. Once it clears the 1,400 level it will be clear that it is starting a brand new stage two bull market. I fully expect the next bull market to be a big one that will take gold prices beyond the 1,900 level. Mining stocks will also go up at an even faster pace than gold. I'll talk about them with you in a later chapter, but the potential in gold investing going forward is huge. Gold and mining stocks are in a stage one base that has been going on for over a year now. This makes right now a great investment buy point, in my opinion.

At the time I am submitting this book for publication, gold is in fact basing in the short-term between $1,290 and $1,350 an ounce. This basing could last a few more days, a few more weeks, or possibly a few more months. A close above $1,350 at this point will probably mean a run straight to $1,400 and beyond. I really cannot predict the exact time and day this current sideways action will end, but it may have ended by the time you are reading this. If so you will know the implications of that. As this book goes to press, it appears that gold is in the process of ending its stage one base and starting a new bull market that will last for several years.

The key is to get in at the end of a stage one basing phase or at the beginning of a new bull market.

The same goes for silver. Take a look at this silver chart and you will see the same basic pattern evident in the chart of gold prices.

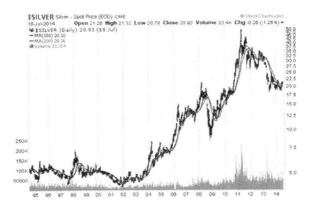

You can see that silver has actually been more volatile than gold over the years. Silver made a peak once it went over $50 an ounce in 2011 at just about the same exact time that gold peaked out. It then went through a stage three topping phase that brought with it a bear market that ended in 2013 with a big drop that took silver prices down below $20 an ounce. Now silver, like gold, is in a stage one basing phase at the time of publication of this book with resistance at the top of this base at $22 an ounce. Once silver closes above this level it will be in a new stage two bull market. Silver and gold tend to actually trade together, with silver being the more volatile of the two. I believe silver is at a good investment buy point just like gold is right now.

In fact, I own both silver and gold investments. Silver and gold are alternative forms of money. They are superior to paper currency as they can never be debased and have been used since the dawn of human civilization. They also are linked to the commodities markets, and tend to go up in times of price inflation and monetary troubles.

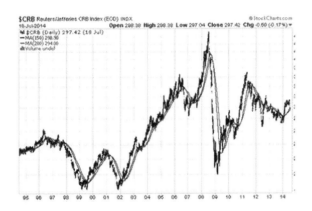

Here is an interesting chart. It's a chart of the Commodity Research Bureau Index, which tracks the price of a basket of commodities, including food and oil. You can see how it has had big swings up and down in the past twenty years. You can also see that it made its last important peak in 2011 and made an important price trend change in 2014. It is in a similar position to gold and silver, which means we are looking at emerging bull markets not just in precious metals, but commodities across the board. That spells inflation.

Now, there is one important thing you must know about bull and bear cycles in financial markets. Although you can easily identify what cycle a market is in by applying stage analysis to a chart, very few people know how to do this. And, even those who know how tend not to apply it, because to use stage analysis requires going against the crowd at critical moments in the financial markets and human psychology makes it difficult for people to do this. To go against the crowd means to face the possible rejection by a person's peers. Most conform to fit in. In many parts of your life it is beneficial for you to fit in and conform, but not when it comes to investing.

The masses look at nothing and know nothing when it comes to investing. All they do is react to the news and the price movements of the past six months and expect them to go on forever. That's why so many of them sell out on bottoms and buy on tops again and again, and never seem to learn. Most are simply incapable of investing at the end of a bear market or at the start of a new bull market, because everyone they know is being negative about investing too. What is worse, usually the TV news says the market is bad after bear market bottoms and it's hard for people to go against what they see and hear on their television sets.

The psychology behind the market has a lot to do with people's perceptions of the market. According to various services that poll investors and advisers, such as Investors Intelligence, most investors are wildly bullish at the tops of bull markets and totally bearish at a bottom, which means most people are always thinking and doing the wrong thing at key points in the cycle of a market. People love tops and hate bottoms.

The reason why is that bear markets are driven by selling. As long as someone holds on to an investment position they tend to be optimistic and bullish or at least hopeful that things will go up for them if they have been declining. But, as a bear market continues they feel more and more pain as it builds up and causes them to doubt. Eventually, the pain gets so bad that they sell. Some sell sooner than others, but bear markets come to an end when all who might sell do so.

What happens to people is that after they sell they become negative on the market. People's brains rationalize their decisions to make people feel like they have done the right thing. So if they get polled after they sold they'll declare themselves to be bears in the belief that the market will fall more after they sold.

The effect of all of this is that widespread bearish sentiment dominates a market after a bear market and often during a stage one basing market as well. The market action causes people to sell. Bull markets actually start after all who can sell do sell, so widespread bearish sentiment is actually a positive for markets.

When a bull market starts almost no one believes it's a bull market, because they have seen so many rallies in the past twelve months and during the previous bear market fail. They don't want to get trapped in another one again so they just don't believe it's real. That's why few people are ever in at the start of a new bull market and the masses are incapable of investing in one. To do so requires going against the crowd and they cannot get themselves to do that.

There is a saying that a bull market climbs a wall of worry, and it's true. What this means is that it takes continued rallies and a long bull market for the worries of the masses to go away and for them to start to believe in the stock market again.

If you look at what happened after the 2008 stock market crash the statistics show that the individual investors in the United States actually sold more stocks than they bought in the first few years of the bull market that began in 2009. Many simply moved money out of stocks and into CD's that paid them practically nothing in fear of another 2008 crash.

It wasn't until the second half of 2013 that the masses started to get back into the US stock market in any meaningful way. By then, the stock market had already gone up for years and had reached a high valuation level. But they didn't care. All they knew was that stocks had now been going up for a long-time so they expected them to keep going higher and they didn't want to miss out. The nightmare of 2008 had finally faded away from their brains and was replaced by a fear of missing out on more gains.

As a result, by January of 2014, over sixty-percent of respondents to the Investors Intelligence survey proclaimed themselves to be bullish on the stock market. This was a level seen the last two times in October of 2007, right at the last bull market top, and a few weeks before the 1987 stock market crash.

Now at the same time, people became extremely bearish on gold and gold stocks in 2013 as they made a bear market bottom that spring. Gold bottomed in 2013, but after that bottom and well into 2014, talking heads on CNBC claimed that gold would keep falling. Just about everyone continued to talk as if gold was still in a giant bear market even though it had already bottomed.

This is common in a stage one base that follows a bear market. Very few people understand the important stages of a stock market and, therefore, do not recognize a stage one base when it is happening. As a result they still think a bear market is going on after it is over.

For example newsletter writer Dennis Gartman is the expert most often interviewed on CNBC when the network wants someone to give an opinion on gold. In May of 2014, gold had a pullback within its stage one base right before it took off to transition into a new bull market. Gartman said on May 27, 2014 on CNBC that the pullback meant that, "gold has broken, it consolidated, and now it's broken again. It's taken out all support." He said he saw no reason to think gold could rally. He argued that it would taken a sudden and unexpected spike in inflation to make gold go up and he didn't "see that happening at this point." Mining stocks quickly surged soon after this report for a 20% gain and have been going up ever since.

Now the thing about Gartman is he is one of the smartest men on CNBC and a real classy guy. For him to get it wrong just at this critical moment shows you how brain controlling the bearish consensus sentiment was at this time. Most guests on CNBC's news reports had been calling for collapses week after week after gold and mining stocks bottomed months before. Gartman was hardly alone. When even the best get caught flat footed due to the domination of mass sentiment you need to take notice. Your brain wants to feel safe and going against the group can put yourself in physical danger in real life situations. So it is hard for people to stand alone at times in the investment world.

It seemed as if no one was bullish at the time. Other experts on CNBC that month said that even if inflation picked up gold would still drop, because they thought that would mean the Federal Reserve would engage in a tight monetary policy that would cause the dollar to rise and hurt gold prices. "I think in the near-term, it's probably going to...break back below $1,300," said Howard Wen, precious metals analyst at HSBC on a CNBC segment that May. "We have CPI tomorrow," he said, "Normally if CPI data is high that would be a positive for gold but that could be a negative because of the Fed's linking of inflation and unemployment to monetary policy. The Fed is concerned about a lack of inflation."

Even people heavily involved in the gold industry were bearish on gold, too. Just as Gartman and Wen were bearish on gold, a senior metals analyst for a giant gold dealer, which sells physical bullion to people, warned of the possibility of more selling to come. "On the one hand, inflation is a positive for gold because it suggests money could flow out of paper assets into hard assets, so that's bullish, but the bearish part of the PPI is it could induce the Fed to continue its tapering on an even more aggressive pace," this expert said on CNBC. It seemed that people thought nothing could make gold go up again.

Bearish talk about gold was all over the internet at this time. On May 29, 2014, Yahoo Finance did a video interview with Steven Pytlar, chief equity strategist at Prime Executions. He predicted a price drop in gold down to between $1,200 to $1,225 an ounce. In another interview, portfolio manager Chad Morganlander of Stifel's Washington Crossing Advisors claimed that the fundamentals agree with Pytlar's call and said of gold that, "it's going to go down." He also recommended that people should sell their gold and use that money to buy into the US stock market and the S&P 500, because "there is a better investment vehicle and that's called equities. We would get away from gold. We would sell it or underweight it and go overweight equities."

Of course, from an investment standpoint, the stock market made no sense at this moment, because it had already been in a bull market for well over five years and had a reached a sky high valuation. But such talk matched the sentiment of the average investor in the United States. Investor surveys showed that investors were heavily bullish on the stock market and bearish on gold too at that time. Many of the Wall Street experts simply told the masses what they wanted to hear, and many of them also fell victim to the consensus crowd psychology themselves.

Within a few weeks of all of these bearish calls gold turned higher. As I write this it is trading between $1,290 and $1,350 an ounce with short-term resistance at $1,350. I believe it is going to go higher - much higher over the next few years - but still many people doubt gold. Few believe that this is the start of a bull market, but once it goes above $1,400 an ounce some who are still in doubt now will start to believe and as it goes higher and higher from there more and more will get on board.

I have been talking about gold and why I think it will go up on my website wallstreetwindow.com. I get emails from people who tell me I am wrong all the time. It seems that in every week that goes by I get an email from someone who forwards me a link to a story, report, or article someone has written somewhere that predicts a drop in gold prices.

How can I believe I am right when so many say I am wrong? Why should you believe gold prices are going to go up? Now, I have told you about financial market cycles and how they apply to gold. A new bull market is starting in precious metals and mining stocks. You can see that the charts show that they are going to go up, but they may not be enough for you. This may be too new of a way of thinking for you and you may need to know what the reason is that they can go up. Let me show you.

CHAPTER II
THE FUNDAMENTAL FACTORS BEHIND GOLD

A lot of people say that gold is going to go up, because they believe that the United States government is going to go bankrupt one day. In reality, it already did years ago. I can tell you the exact moment it happened. The date this happened was on August, 15, 1971. What happened on that day?

Well, a lot of events led to that moment. In order to tell you the story behind that day you must understand that the United States became the most powerful nation in the world after World War II. The rest of the world got bombed out by that war and had to rebuild. Japan was devastated and so were Europe and Russia. But the US was not hurt. It came out of the war in a position of economic and military dominance.

In terms of military power, the United States dropped two atomic bombs on Japan. These were the most powerful weapon detonations ever used in the history of warfare and the US was the only nation in the world with such weapons at that time. As a result, the United States now had the most powerful military ever seen in human history.

The United States also came out of the war in a position of great economic power. With its factories still intact, it became a great exporter to the rest of the world. It was also a lender of money to the rest of the world. In the years following the war, it created global economic institutions such as the International Monetary Fund and the World Bank. It helped create the United Nations, and it is no coincidence that the UN headquarters was built in New York City.

After World War II, the United States evolved from being a continental republic into being a global empire. In the next few decades, the nation became something much different from what the founding fathers created. Before World War II, the United States never had a large permanent standing army and hardly anyone paid any income taxes. The government didn't need much tax revenue, because it was small in size.

But in the years following World War II, the United States became involved in the Cold War. So it kept its new big army and turned the "War Department" into the "Department of Defense." It created a Central Intelligence Agency to covertly intervene in smaller nations throughout the world and keep them on the right side. Black ops, black bag money campaigns, and even assassination programs became a part of what CIA people called "the great game."

The United States became involved in an expensive nuclear arms race against the Soviet Union. Defense spending exploded and a new military-industrial complex rose in the United States. A new "power elite" emerged behind the scenes that came to make most of the big decisions when it came to war and peace and foreign affairs. The

United States government had a "national security state" within it that grew in immense power. The federal government became a big government warfare/welfare state with giant expenditures that required big taxes and eventually big debts.

I tell the story of how this all happened from 1945 until 1963 in my book *The War State*. If you have not read it yet then you should read it after you read this book. Today you'll find that when you factor in the interest on the national debt from past wars plus total defense expenditures that United States spends almost 40% of its federal budget on the military. It accounts for over 46% of total world arms spending.

The American defense department employees more people on the planet than any other enterprise on earth with 3.2 million American employees. To give you an idea of how big this is, the second largest employer inside the United States is Wal-Mart with 2.1 million employees and after that is Mc-Donald's with 1.9 million people working for it. So a good portion of the American economy is dependent on the defense industry and the big government jobs tied to it, which creates a big burden on the private sector of the economy. These defense contractors receive no bid guaranteed cost plus contracts from the government and therefore do not act inside the free market price forces created by supply and demand, but feed off the productivity of others.

As he left office President Eisenhower gave a famous farewell address in which he said, "We must guard against the acquisition of unwarranted influence, whether sought or unsought, by the military-industrial complex. The potential for the disastrous rise of misplaced power exists and will persist." Today these words seem timeless.

What people really remember Ike saying is, "We must never let the weight of this combination endanger our liberties or democratic processes. We should take nothing for granted. Only an alert and knowledgeable citizenry can compel the proper meshing of the huge industrial and military machinery of defense with our peaceful methods and goals, so that security and liberty may prosper together."

What most people take away from this speech is a warning that the military-industrial complex could "endanger our liberties or democratic processes." However, in other speeches and in released records of private White House meetings, President Eisenhower expressed worries over the size of defense spending as being the real grave danger that would lead to great harm to liberties and democracy in the United States.

President Eisenhower worried that if the government spent more than it took in that it could end up running a big enough budget deficit to send the country "straight toward inflation of an uncontrollable character." That would mean the government would have to interfere in the private market to try to control inflation and keep defense spending going at the same time. The whole nation could become a warped "garrison state" as a result.

Eisenhower thought that anyone who didn't see this as a danger and understand "that national security and national solvency are mutually dependent, and that permanent maintenance of a crushing weight of military power would eventually create dictatorship, should not be entrusted with any kind of responsibility in our country." In one of his final cabinet meetings he asked, "Can free government overcome the many demands made by special interests and the indulgence of selfish motives?" Would the interests of the war state come to dominate the economy and warp American institutions and government? Today, we are used to see-ing giant budget deficits and people telling us not to worry about them. Vice-President Dick Cheney famously made the statement that "deficits don't matter" to Treasury Secre-tary Paul O'Neill who kept bugging him about them. But in the 1940's, 1950's and 1960's, Presidents Roosevelt, Truman, Eisenhower, and Kennedy all kept their eye on the budget and fought against the creation of big government spending deficits. They had to.

After World War the United States II created a mon-etary system that made the US dollar the reserve currency of the world that also put a lid on the growth of government spending deficits. It was called the Bretton Woods system and it made the United States the economic center of the world for decades by linking the US dollar to gold in the international currency markets.

The British Empire had linked the pound to gold during its time of world dominance and other nations followed its lead. But the debts of World War I and the Great Depres-sion ended the world gold standard. In the closing months of World War II, leaders from across the world met in Bret-ton Woods, New Hampshire to hammer out a new global monetary system.

Each nation agreed to tie the value of their currencies to the US dollar. To bolster faith in the dollar, the US agreed separately to link the dollar to gold at the rate of $35 per ounce of gold. At this price foreign governments and central banks were able to exchange dollars for gold.

Bretton Woods established a system of payments based on the dollar, in which all currencies were defined in rela-tion to the dollar, itself convertible into gold, and above all, "as good as gold." The US currency was now effectively the world currency, the standard to which every other currency was pegged. As the world's key currency, most international transactions were denominated in US dollars.

The effect of this was that the US dollar was the currency with the most purchasing power and it was the only currency that was backed by gold. Additionally, all European nations that had been involved in World War II were highly in debt and transferred large amounts of gold into the United States, a fact that contributed to its world supremacy. Thus, the US dollar strongly appreciated in the rest of the world and, therefore, became the key currency of the Bretton Woods system.

The strong value of the US dollar helped the United States import goods at a cheaper price than other nations were able to do. It also made it easier to sell government debt in the form of Treasury bonds on the world market. After World War II, the United States actually ran giant trade surpluses as it exported manufacturing goods to the rest of the world. This helped to create a shortage of dollars in the world. One result was that the Truman administration launched the "Marshall Plan" to send aid to Europe to help it rebuild.

Bretton Woods and the end of World War II helped created a post-war boom in the American economy. A housing boom took off across the nation and so did a new boom in car manufacturing. President Eisenhower built a national highway system and a new consumer culture was born. The middle class grew and people felt very confident about the future.

But in time, a problem emerged. The Bretton Woods system put a limit on how much debt a nation could accumulate, because it demanded that dollars could be exchanged for gold in the international currency markets. To tell you how this worked, before Bretton Woods, the gold standard was used to back currencies. So the international value of currency was determined by its fixed relationship to gold and gold was used to settle international accounts. The gold standard maintained fixed exchange rates that were seen as desirable because they reduced the risk when trading with other countries.

Imbalances in international trade were theoretically rectified automatically by the gold standard. A country with a growing trade deficit and growing debts would have depleted gold reserves and would thus have to reduce its money supply. The resulting fall in demand would reduce imports and the lowering of prices would boost exports; thus the deficit would be rectified. Any country experiencing inflation would lose gold and, therefore, would have a decrease in the amount of money available to spend.

Eventually, this decrease in the amount of money would act to reduce the inflationary pressure. In effect, what the gold standard did was keep monetary order by limiting the amount of disorder government spending deficits and trade deficits could create. It acted as a brake on debt accumulation and government spending.

In theory, the new Bretton Woods system could do the same thing. And it did for a period of time. And it was during this time that the United States became great. But then, several things began to happen that caused people in Europe and Asia to slowly begin to transfer their dollars into gold. The United States began to generate small, but meaningful, trade and budget deficits.

Europe and Japan also began to rebuild themselves. Right after World War II, the US manufactured half of the world's goods. However, as they rebuilt their factories they began to export to the United States. But Presidents Eisenhower and Kennedy were able to make some small adjustments here and there that stopped the gold outflow.

The Johnson Presidency, though, ruined the nation's fiscal position. President Lyndon Johnson created big government spending deficits when he launched the Vietnam War and his social spending "war on poverty" programs he called the Great Society. He vastly increased government expenditures and did not raise taxes. The result was a deterioration in the position of the US trade deficit and an outflow of gold. The US economy grew, but inflation picked up and imbalances built up. Lyndon Johnson's response, and that of his successor President Nixon, was to pressure the US Federal Reserve into simply printing more money.

Both Presidents refused to make tough decisions. They did not demand that the American people tighten their belts and pay up for the Vietnam War and their social spending programs so foreign creditors simply demanded more of the nation's gold. What started as a trickle of gold flowing out of the nation became a tidal wave.

If all of the gold left the nation, than the US dollar would become worthless. The nation, in effect, was heading to bankruptcy, because it could not stop the gold outflow without raising taxes, reducing spending, and running a budget surplus. No Republican or Democrat wanted to do that so Nixon made a decision with a few of his closest advisors in secret. He did not even tell anyone in the US State Department. He decided to announce unilaterally to the world that the United States would no longer allow people to convert dollars into gold. He would shut the gold window.

He would make the US dollar a pure paper currency backed by nothing. The thing is, he wasn't sure what would happen. He was desperate. One of the men who helped create this plan for President Nixon even told him that they did not know what would happen after Nixon announced it, but he had to do it anyway. Nixon made the announcement on TV on August 15, 1971 by stating that the government would abandon the Bretton Woods agreements and no longer link the US dollar to the price of gold.

What came as a result was nine years of monetary chaos. Gold had been fixed to the dollar at $35 an ounce. Gold prices soared until they briefly went to $850 an ounce in 1980. During this time, inflation in the United States exploded and the economy went into a recession. Two years after Bretton Woods the annual inflation rate hit 8%. By 1980, it was at 14%. At the same time, the stock market went nowhere so stock investors lost their ass thanks to inflation. OPEC put on an oil embargo that helped to drive gas prices up too. People who lived through this time remember this as the miserable Carter years of stagflation.

Toward the end of Jimmy Carter's presidency it became clear that someone had to do something to stop the inflation. Federal Reserve Chairman, Paul Volker, took action and jammed up interest rates to 20%. This, of course, caused a big recession in the first year of Ronald Reagan's Presidency. Housing markets got smashed and many people in debt went bankrupt. Small farmers got wiped out.

But eventually, the situation stabilized. The high interest rates caused gold prices to fall and inflation fell close to zero. Other nations followed the lead of the United States and simply floated their currencies on the world market too. Now currencies fluctuated in value. Now the United States no longer needed gold to finance its deficits. It could simply print money out of thin air.

However, the United States was still the biggest economy in the world with the biggest military machine ever seen in human history. So, without any other nation going back to a gold standard, the US dollar still maintained its dominance. Paul Volker's actions brought confidence, and once he finished defeating inflation and began to lower rates, a new economic boom took place in the United States. President Ronald Reagan cut taxes and people were happy.

But, as the years went by, two things happened underneath the surface prosperity. Pure fiat currency leads to sickness. First, financial speculation came to dominate the economy. A monetary system based on money printing created wild gyrations in financial markets all over the world that speculators were able to take advantage of. A giant secular stock market boom was one result. If you look at a chart of the United States stock market since its inception and you'll see that its rate of advance accelerated in the 1980's. It went on a slow upward slope in the 1800's with lots of ups and downs and continued higher on a slow trajectory until 1980. Then it began to go up at a parabolic rate. The reason was not because the U.S. economy was suddenly growing faster than it ever had before in history, but because the collapse of Bretton Woods and a pure paper currency helped contribute to money printing and speculation that helped create an accelerating stock market boom.

A bull market culture in equities grew. A decade of captivating gains brought the masses into the stock market in the 1990's. They believed in the market. Big debts led to big trade imbalances. Manufacturing in the United States shrank, but the finance sector grew. By 2003, 40% of corporate profits were generated in the finance industry.

Debt troubles came though. Paper currency debts enabled nations and companies to use debt to grow and profit. One debt crises after another erupted periodically in third world nations as hot speculative finance went in and out of places such as Mexico and Argentina. Even South Korea suffered from one.

A debt crisis also hit the Savings and Loan industry in the United States around 1990. Financial volatility grew. One result was the 1987 stock market crash. Another was the internet bubble of the 1990's and 2000 stock market bust. Another was a real estate bubble that grew in the last decade and the stock market crash of 2008.

The crash of 2008 brought heavily indebted Wall Street banks to the edge of bankruptcy. To stop that the Federal Reserve and Treasury Department created a bailout program, giving banks over a trillion dollars. As a result, the United States budget deficit exploded to a trillion dollars in 2008 and the Federal Reserve took toxic junk debts off the books of bankers and put them on its own balance sheets.

Wall Street won and the stock market went back up, but the US economy has been in a horrible recession ever since. The middle class lost a lot of its wealth and as a whole has shrunk. Dependency on government programs such as food stamps and unemployment benefits on the part of the masses is now just a regular part of everyday life for millions of Americans. The United States has become more of a two-class society, but corporate profits for financial companies and companies well connected to the government have exploded over the past few years.

This is a lot of history you probably already knew, but when you sit back and put everything in context you see there are two key things to take away from it. First, the end of Bretton Woods on August 15, 1971, was a turning point in the history of the United States and the American economy. It was the only way to keep the out of control big government warfare/welfare system going.

Deficit spending became the only way to fund the Reagan defense boom and the war on terror and the welfare programs without putting big taxes on people. It was the only way to keep piling up big debts. And people came to not only like the system, but many came to love it, because they benefited from rising housing prices and rising stock market prices. The so called one-percent got richer and many in the middle class saw the equity bull market as a way to get rich too. So, when the crash of 2008 came few asked any questions. And few have protested ever since. Few worry about the growth of government and such things as NSA spy programs, because so many benefit from government action in the form of government spending or money printing. Democrats and Republicans alike have come to love their leaders and to worship big brother in their own way.

Going off Bretton Woods caused economic turmoil, but also enabled the United States to create debt with pure paper money. It helped create a financialization of the economy. Business leaders in the US used to be leaders of manufacturing such as Henry Ford and invention like Thomas Edison. Now, they are faceless men working in Wall Street offices creating nothing tangible, but using debt generation and speculation to generate profits with losses socialized by the government. People like Jamie Dimon are now held up as economic heroes on CNBC.

But just as Bretton Woods came to an end due to too much debt, this current monetary system of paper dollar dominance can come to an end too. The result would be financial turmoil that would be like the 1970's on steroids. You would get inflation growth and an explosion in gold and commodity prices. In the 1970's gold went from $35 an ounce to a peak of $887 an ounce. A similar gain in gold from its low around $250 an ounce in 1999 would take gold prices up to well over $6,000 an ounce. Gold and silver bugs would thrive and, of course, make fortunes.

The system is already breaking down, but what would really cause it to come to an end is if people once against lost confidence in the dollar in the international currency markets. They would do that if they began to worry about the size of the growing government debt and its annual budget deficit. We have seen such situations happen twice in Argentina in the past fourteen years and most recently in Greece and Cyprus. Something similar could happen in the United States if the nation entered a full-blown government debt crisis.

In effect, by bailing out Wall Street banks in 2008 and taking on their debts, the US government and the Federal Reserve turned a crisis for Wall Street into a potential government debt crisis that all Americans could have to pay for. But, so far, there has been no government debt crisis even though the debts are growing. When will they matter?

The Congressional Budget Office(CBO) projects that if nothing is done to control the budget deficit then by 2030 the United States will face a frightening current account deficit of over 15%. Historically, when a nation reaches a current account deficit over 5% its runs into a financial crisis. A level of 6% preceded the 2008 stock market crash.

To put it to you another way, in 2009, the net debt of the United States government was $50.7 trillion. This was debt owned by households, corporations, and central banks all over the world. The CBO has projected two scenarios for US debt. In the first scenario, in which Washington takes steps to control the size of debt by cutting spending and raising taxes, the debt held by the public would be at 52% of GDP in 2037. In the second scenario, in which nothing is done, the debt to GDP ratio would reach 199% in the same timeframe.

Such a level would create a fiscal crisis for the United States, because the CBO projects that at that point just the mandatory spending programs for the federal government would exceed its revenue. You can see this in the following chart put together by the US Treasury and made available by the Government Accounting Office.

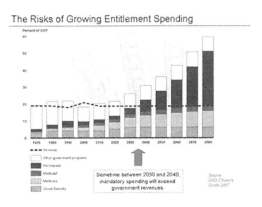

If government expenses exceed revenue at some point the budget would hit a point of no return, because as debt grows the cost of financing debt grows too thanks to rising interest payment demands. That would mean big trouble.

As of today, there is no sign that either political party is serious about doing anything about this, or that they are willing to work together to find a solution. No one has been able to lead and make the tough decisions. The Republican and Democratic parties gather the support of voters by existing in opposition to one another, but both parties feed off of the campaign donations of corporate sponsors that are dependent on government financing.

Democrats portray themselves as friends of the little people while receiving most of their campaign financing from Wall Street international bankers, such as Goldman Sachs. Meanwhile the neoconservatives in the Republican Party claim to be for smaller government while they push for reckless wars and ever-expanding defense budgets that drive more money into the coffers of the defense contractors, such as Lockheed Martin, who fund them. So, we have a stagnating economy with growing inflation, growing government that snuffs out private capital investment, and the dangerous expansion of government debt. It's a demonic combination.

What the parties offer the party follower is a symbolic identity. By pledging their loyalty to one of the two parties they get to feel like they are a part of a team, but they get nothing of real substance from their pledge. The party leaders do not talk to you and are not going to help you. They serve their own master. You must help yourself. All you have to do is look at the back of a US dollar bill and reject the false enlightenment represented by the pyramid eye symbol printed on to it. The kingdom of God is within you. Gold may not represent spiritual salvation, but it is your financial salvation.

The politicians have failed us and the US seems to be a nation lacking in leaders. Everyone knows there is trouble brewing in the distance. The CBO projections are talked about at times in the media and in the mainstream financial press, but there is something you need to know about them.

They are based on an assumption so flawed that it makes them practically a fraud. The situation is much worse than most people realize. People inside the Federal Reserve though do know. Time is running out. Instead of decades to go we may have only a few years left to go.

In August of 2007, Frederick Mishkin, who had been appointed to the Federal Reserve Board of Governors by Ben Bernanke - the two have been close friends for decades - wrote a report for the Fed that laid out what would happen to the economy if real estate prices in the United States were to drop and what the Federal Reserve should do if it starts to happen.

The paper called for a rapid reduction in interest rates to near zero. The report predicted everything that was to come. I got a hold of it in September 2007, and after I read it I realized that the US economy and stock market were in big trouble. With this knowledge, I actually bet against the stock market in 2008 and made a gain of over 35% in my main account as the stock market crashed and almost everyone else lost tons of money in it.

It was one of the most important papers I have read in my life, and as soon as I read it I shared it with all of the people I could on my WallStreetWindow website.

Today, Fred Mishkin no longer serves on the Federal Reserve Board, but he and a team of economists presented another paper back in February, 2013, at a Federal Reserve policy conference titled "Crunch Time: Fiscal Crises and the Role of Monetary Policy." In this report they predict another financial crisis in a few years - this time to be centered around a government funding debt disaster - if nothing is done.

So far, at publication time of this book, no American mainstream reporter has done a story about the report. CNBC has not informed its viewers about it and as far as I can tell there has not been any mention of it even in the Wall Street Journal.

Of course, I do not recall CNBC sharing with their audience the 2007 Mishkin report so it's no surprise that they aren't telling their audience about this one either. Journalists in the United States are asleep and TV news is just propaganda. I can't find a single story about it anywhere. I have a link to the report in a post I did about it on my website. If you want to read the whole thing just type "wallstreetwindow crunch time" in Google search and you can find my post.

Now, despite the seeming press blackout, this was a hot topic of discussion inside the Federal Reserve in 2013. At the end of February 2013, a panel convened at the Fed's "U.S. Monetary Policy Forum" in Chicago to talk just about the report. Mishkin then presented a revised version of the report in August of 2013 at the annual Jackson Hole Fed gathering.

The report begins with an abstract summary of what is to come in the rest of its 94 pages. The summary contains these lines:

"We analyze the recent experience of advanced economies using both econometric methods and case studies and conclude that countries with debt above 80% of GDP and persistent current-account deficits are vulnerable to a rapid fiscal deterioration as a result of these tipping-point dynamics. Such feedback is left out of current long-term U.S. budget projections and could make it much more difficult for the U.S. to maintain a sustainable budget course. A potential fiscal crunch also puts fundamental limits on what monetary policy is able to achieve. In simulations of the Federal Reserve's balance sheet, we find that under our baseline assumptions, in 2017-18 the Fed will be running sizable income losses on its portfolio net of operating and other expenses and therefore for a time will be unable to make remittances to the U.S. Treasury. Under alternative scenarios that allow for an emergence of fiscal concerns, the Fed's net losses would be more substantial."

The study goes on to look at the history of financial government debt crises in countries all over the world and finds that when the ratio of government debt to GDP passes the 80% mark, eventually some sort of crisis hits. These crisis can hit suddenly when the costs to finance government deficits increases exponentially due to a rise in interest rates. Then governments can no longer manage their debts and must default or print them away. This isn't really new stuff. A great book came out a few years ago, titled *This Time Is Different*, by a group of economists who studied all of this using historic economic data from countries all over the world and broke down the various ways these debt blow ups tend to play out. This "Crunch Time" report uses this book as a source. It's worth reading too.

Now as I have mentioned, based on CBO projections twenty-five years from now, and sometime around 2030-2037, has been the mainstream target for seeing a future of debt trouble for the United States. In the last chapter of my book *The War State*(you can find it on Amazon too), I cite a Peter Peterson article in the foreign policy journal <u>Foreign Affairs</u> where he uses these CBOE figures and targets the same time period around 2030 as our window of trouble.

However, once you get to page 47 of the Mishkin "Crunch Time" report, you get to the scary stuff. If you find it on the internet and read it for yourself you'll see that the CBO figures people are using in these projections are based on the faulty assumption that interest rates will stay at their current historically low near zero levels forever. If rates go up than the costs of funding the government debt would suddenly rise exponentially - the government debt to GDP will then skyrocket well above the 100% crisis level overnight. Investors all over the world would demand a higher rate of interest to fund the country's national debt, the dollar would decline, and another economic crisis worse than the one of 2008 would hit the United States as the cost for the federal government and the Federal Reserve to finance the debt escalates.

As this "Crunch Time" report states:

"In 2012, debt service was quite low (less than 1.4% of GDP) because interest rates were so low. Roughly one-quarter of the Treasury debt outstanding is in the bill sector (meaning an original maturity of 1 year or less) and borrowing costs at the short end of the yield curve have been close to zero for the past several years. Even longer-term notes and bonds issued by the Treasury in recent years have had a very low coupon. But, if the U.S. continues to pile on more debt and if we assume – as CBO (2013) does – a normalization of interest rates over the course of coming years (to roughly 4.0% for 3-month T-bills and 5.2% for 10-year notes), then debt service costs will eventually skyrocket."

To put this in simple terms, if the interest rate on the 10-year treasury bond were to go to over 5.2% than the cost to finance the deficit will explode.

The report states:

"The CBO's baseline estimates (and similar projections produced by the White House Office of Management and Budget) assume that long-term interest rates rise gradually to reach a level of 5.2% in 2018 and then remain constant at that level despite a continued escalation in the amount of public debt outstanding. The theoretical analysis and historical experience reviewed in Sections 2 and 3 suggest that this assumption could lead to a significant understatement of the potential deterioration in the budget picture because yields are assumed to hold steady at normalized levels as debt continues to accumulate."

The implications of all of this means that the Federal Reserve cannot allow the interest rate on the 10-year Treasury bond to rise beyond 5.2%. To prevent that it would have to increase its so-called "quantitative easing" bond buying program or come up with another one with a new name and purchase more bonds if rates start to rise. The report calls this policy "fiscal dominance" and a way to manage the mushrooming debt "through inflation."

The report explains:

"To see how this would play out in practice, we need to recognize that fiscal dominance puts a central bank between a rock and a hard place. If the central bank does not monetize the debt, then interest rates on the government debt will rise sharply, causing the economy to contract. Indeed, without monetization, fiscal dominance may result in the government defaulting on its debt, which would lead to a severe financial disruption, producing an even more severe economic contraction. Hence, the central bank will in effect have little choice and will be forced to purchase the government debt and monetize it, eventually leading to a surge in inflation."

All of this means that the Federal Reserve cannot allow interest rates for the ten year Treasury bond to go above 5.2%. In order to prevent rates going over 5.2%, the Fed would have to print money like mad if they approached that level. The implications are that we face inflationary pressures, a falling dollar, and the potential for a new crisis by 2018. It would be a historic turning point just like Nixon taking the dollar off the gold standard in 1971 proved to be.

Such an event could mark the final chapter of the era of US dollar global supremacy. It is an era that began after World War II and was backed by the fact that the US dollar became the reserve currency of the world. It has enabled the federal government to essentially run gigantic deficits to fund its military-industrial complex and various social programs.

For investors, the result would be financial turmoil in the stock markets all over the world, and particularly in the United States. You can expect to see the DOW and S&P 500 make some wild swings that wipe a lot of people out. Bonds would not act as a safe haven like they did in 2008. Instead, gold would.

Now you may think all of this is dire and extreme. The fact of the matter is that gold is starting a new bull market and the charts suggest there is tremendous upside to come for gold. Is gold factoring in a dire future to come or just going up in a fun bull market? We cannot be sure, and yes we cannot predict the future.

But, we do not need to. Whatever happens whoever is aligned in the correct big trends will build wealth no matter what happens to everything else. So we just need to know the big trend and the big trend in the markets right now is that we have new bull markets in gold and commodities beginning in front of us that will likely last at least three to five years, because that is the average amount of time a bull market lasts.

In such a scenario the investments aligned correctly to take advantage of such a trend will enable those positioned right to multiply their wealth. And if you are reading this in 2015 you probably still got time to get in the game. Even in 2016 it may not be too late, but the earlier you get in the better. What is the best way to play this trend?

CHAPTER III
HOW TO PROFIT FROM THIS GOLD BULL MARKET

The safest way to invest in precious metals is simply to buy gold bullion and silver from a reputable precious metals dealer. Then you need to go put them in a safe place that you only tell a few people who need to know. You do not want to just store them in your house! You need someplace secret and safe.

Whether you buy coins or bars is up to you. Most people like a mix of both. I consider my bullion holdings as the safest part of my overall investment portfolio. I think of it as my real Fort Knox.

Inside my brokerage account, I buy gold and silver through exchange traded funds that hold both. I also invest in stocks through such funds too. The symbols of the funds I use are GLD, SLV, GDX, and GDXJ. I am not just a gold bug though. I have bought traditional investments in the US stock market at times and invested in foreign stocks too. There is a time and place for everything.

Although I have been investing in the stock market since the 1990's, starting in 2002 I have been an investor in gold bullion and a trader in gold mining stocks. At the beginning of 2002, I came to conclude that gold and commodities were about to start a big bull market. Since then I have bought and sold out of my positions several times as we have seen several bull and bear markets occur in the gold market since 2002, but at the time of writing this book I believe we are about to see the biggest bull market in gold ever over the next few years.

However, I consider my investments outside of gold bullion to be more speculative in a nature. Mining stocks as a whole tend to be more volatile than gold bullion and can be individually impacted in both positive and negative ways to specific company news. It is not unusual to see gold prices go up and then shares of an individual gold company go down, because it had to announce bad news. It may be a negative earnings release or a need to do a secondary offering to raise money by selling more stock, thereby diluting current shareholders, that hits the stock.

However, the right gold stocks will rise exponentially as the gold bull market continues. Higher risks means the potential for higher rewards.

One good and bad thing about buying gold stocks and exchange traded funds that invest in gold is that you have instant liquidity. If you want to take your investment out all you have to do is call your stock broker and get out at the quoted market price. If you trade online you don't even have to do that. You can just turn on your computer, connect to the internet and type! But easy trades makes it easier to make mistakes.

With gold bullion and coins, you have to find a gold dealer or another individual who is willing to purchase your gold. It's an extra step. If you decide to sell your gold then you have to package your physical gold up and mail it to a dealer or else get in your car and take it to someone.

This can actually be a good thing. Most people who try to trade in and out of gold actually make mistakes. If things go up for a few months they get tempted to sell and then end up left behind when the market goes up without them or else they worry during little corrections and sell on bottoms. So having a nice core Fort Knox position in gold bullion that isn't as easy to sell as pressing a button is good, because it means you'll be less likely to make the mistake of selling out too soon. You'll learn not to worry about it and to just enjoy holding on to it. Most people who own stocks look at the trading quotes all of the time, get stressed out over little gyrations, and mess up.

That said, though, the right gold stocks have the potential to go up even more than the price of gold does over the next few years. You see, the profits that mining companies generate during a gold bull market are tremendous, because when the price of gold moves up their profits explode exponentially. For example, if the price of gold rises from $1,300 to $1,560 an ounce that represents a 20% increase. To show you what this means, right now it costs a gold company on average $1,200 to get an ounce of gold out of the ground. A gold price of $1,300 translates into a profit of $100 at a $1,200 cost. This means that a 20% move in the price of gold from $1,300 to $1,560 translates into an over 500% increase in profits for the gold company.

This gives a gold investor tremendous leverage for his investment dollars and gold stocks tend to rise by a much larger percentage than the price of gold itself during a gold bull market. In fact, the gains can be astronomical, which is what first brought my interest to mining stocks. That should be no surprise because when the profits of a company increase rapidly big stock gains almost always follow.

Mining stocks are essentially leveraged investments in gold and silver. That is why they can go up more than gold does at times and can also crash to nothing too. When the last giant bull market in gold came to an end in 1980, most gold stocks actually went to zero - the companies went bankrupt! After that a few dozen of the biggest companies came to dominate the industry for the next few decades.

THE GOLD INDUSTRY

Back in 2002, when I realized that the opportunities to profit in the gold bull market were going to become a once in a lifetime opportunity that I had to take advantage of, I didn't know anything about gold! I knew a lot about stocks and financial markets, but gold was a whole world unto itself.

So, I realized that I needed to make contacts with gold analysts, newsletter writers, and management teams. I wanted to know what makes the gold community tick so that I could build off of their advice and get access to the private market place. I was determined to make money in gold and decided that I needed to meet and befriend some real gold experts who could bring me up to speed.

So I started to travel to mining industry shows across the United State and Canada. Most of them were organized in the same fashion. They rent out a conference center and divide it up into two sections. In the first section, there are speaker panels and smaller workshops where you can get one-on-one attention. In the second section, there is almost always an exhibition hall with booths.

These booths were made up of brokers, companies making trading software, and small cap companies trying to attract investor interest. Despite the dozen or so major gold conferences a year, in reality the gold community is small.

When I first started attending these conferences, very little money was actually flowing into gold companies, even though the stocks were going higher. The simple fact of the matter is that gold and the gold stocks are only a small segment of the financial world. At the start of 2001, the combined market cap for all publicly traded gold stocks was less than the market cap of Disney.

As I write this, Wall Street is still shunning them. Mainstream investors and CNBC talking heads have not accepted the fact that gold is in a bull market and the last bear market cycle that ended in 2013 has made most small market players skeptical of the start of this new bull market. They still think that the gold rally will fail and are afraid to commit money to it. This is why the small gold companies still use private investors for financing and depend on newsletters and investment conferences for exposure.

On one hand, this is a good thing. You can make contacts with the leaders of the gold industry yourself and most gold companies are very accommodating toward individual investors. This is a virtual impossibility right now in sectors such as technology. You would have a difficult time trying to meet Bill Gates or Larry Ellison at an investment conference, but you can meet Robert McEwen, who helped to build Gold-

Corp into a company with a market cap of over $22 billion at a gold conference.

On the other hand, many tiny gold companies are nothing but pieces of paper and their reliance on small newsletter writers for exposure is a sign of their lack of investment merit. In fact, many of them border on being outright frauds.

When I started to go to investment conferences that featured gold companies, I made it a point to have private conversations with the gold CEO's to get a better feel for the industry. I spent one night with one of them on a $3.5 million dollar yacht watching football and drinking beer. Loose lips are more revealing.

I took a liking to this guy and he seemed straight to me. Of course, he believed that gold would go up, but he also warned me that 80% of the small cap exploration companies are "fake." He has a 25-year background in the industry and knows most of the key players. The analysts don't follow the stocks so all you have are newsletter writers. I asked him, "who can the small investors rely on?"

He laughed and said that most of them are bought off with stock. He told me of one or two that were good, but then added, "you need to understand that they need to make a living."

He went on to tell me that when it comes to exploration companies it is all about promotion. His words made comments that I heard from another CEO of a small exploration company earlier that day come to mind. During that previous conversation, with this dude, he made a sly remark to the effect that gold exploration companies are the best companies to run, because the balance sheet doesn't matter.

Earnings do not matter. The CEO of this small exploration company said that people do not know how to value your properties and it is all about its unknown potential and the "psychology" of gold.

The last time I heard CEO's say that their earnings didn't matter was during the internet stock mania of 1999. Those stocks flew and crashed to nothing. When the gold bull is over most of the small cap gold stocks will go back to nothing too. However, before then you will eventually see bunches of new companies appear out of nowhere and have their moment in the sun.

I got the impression from both men that stock promotion is central to the small junior mining and gold exploration stocks. The man on the yacht point blank told me that it is not the shares of companies with the best prospects that go up the most, but the ones with the heaviest promotion that do. The way he put it, if you have good properties and no promotion the stock will lag, but if you have crap properties and heavy promotion it will fly as gold goes higher. And, if you have both good properties and heavy promotion than you can have a rocket.

The easiest way for people to promote a gold stock is to get newsletter writers involved, especially those that specialize in the gold market. They are the people who can directly reach potential investors. Promoters get them involved by allowing them to buy stock at steep discounts on the private market, paying them money, or by simply giving them shares.

One of the most popular ways to promote a stock is to send out mass mail flyers to investors in the mail. These fliers almost always feature a newsletter writer, who supposedly has earned his subscribers unbelievable profits, and a write up for the company that it should go up 1000% or even more. That write up is the real purpose of the mailing. The newsletter writer is just there to give it credibility.

The problem is that more often than not the investor who buys on these mailings is buying in near a top. The promoter, the newsletter writer, and everyone else involved in pumping the stock already got in way before the flier is sent out. After the last sucker gets in the stock almost always goes back down. You see with no earnings or real prospects they have nowhere else to go. It's like the movie "Boiler Room." If you haven't seen it you might enjoy it. It's a good popcorn movie.

Just so you know, I do not engage in any of these promotional activities. I am not paid to promote stocks. In the gold industry, it is rare to find a newsletter writer who isn't involved in this sort of activity. I've even heard of one writer calling the gold companies himself and asking them how much they will pay him to write up their stock! Luckily there are ways that you can determine whether or not a newsletter writer is doing real analysis or is just giving you a sales pitch. And there are, indeed, a few top-notch analysts out there.

There is a simple way to separate the wheat from the chaff. Anyone who recommends a stock must put a disclosure with their recommendation if they already own shares, or were given stock, or paid cash by the company or a third-party. Read the writer's disclaimer very carefully to find this disclosure. If they simply own shares that they bought, that is one thing, but if they are being compensated to promote the stock be very wary of what you are reading, because it is not an unbiased piece of research.

As time goes on, I expect these conflicts of interest to become a big issue. Investor awareness will increase. I just hope that it won't take a scandal for it to start. For now, you must carefully choose which newsletters you follow. Make sure they are being written by real independent analysts and aren't just tout sheets.

I learned from talking to these CEO's that I needed to be careful in what I invest in. I needed to learn for myself what is the best way to evaluate a gold or silver company. I put lots of my own money into work in the market and I want to buy the best stocks, not just ones that are going up because everything else is, or because they are being promoted. If you are going to buy into a basket of gold stocks you should just buy the best ones.

TYPES OF GOLD STOCKS

The trick is to determine which gold stocks have real potential. The safest gold stocks are the large producing gold companies. Every collection of gold stocks should revolve around a core holding in a few of the largest producers. These companies include AngloGold, Barrick Gold, and Newmont Mining among others. They are the stocks that are the institutional favorites of mutual fund managers. In fact, if the gold bull market continues the way that I expect it will then Newmont will become a must own stock, much like Cisco Systems was in the 1990's. Yes, at the time of this writing I own some of these stocks directly and all of them through gold stock exchange traded funds.

Generally speaking, the higher the potential gain the higher the risk that an investor takes in a stock. Higher returns are available to gold investors from mid-tier producing gold companies that mine anywhere from 100,000 to 1,000,000 ounces of gold a year. These stocks have smaller share floats so it takes less money flowing into the stock to make it go up in value. The companies have at least one producing mine and often own several mines, some of which may have higher production costs and were closed during the last gold bear market. As the price of gold advances, these mines reopen to provide a boost to the company's profits. A lot of these companies end up getting bought out. Bema Gold, Wheaton River, and Cambior were all mid-tier producers who were bought out at huge prices.

Mid-tier mining companies can become takeover targets and often engage in gold exploration activities. Often, they join smaller exploration companies in developing potential mines. Mid-tier mining companies are very dependent on the price of gold and often take on debt to develop mining properties. As a result, if the gold price drops they often have to scramble to raise more capital, which means diluting shareholders or floating more debt, and some of them often become insolvent during gold bear markets.

Below the large and mid-tier producers are exploration and junior mining companies, which make up most of the gold companies on the exchanges. Exploration companies consist of only a couple of employees, most of whom are geologists, who search for new gold deposits in hopes of finding the next big discovery. They raise money to purchase claims on properties. Their shares are penny stocks and are akin to lottery tickets. Only one in a thousand pay off in the end. Of course the reward when one of these companies hits pay dirt is enormous, but for every one of these stocks that become big winners hundreds become zeros.

Junior mining companies try to transform exploration properties into producing mines. Some junior mining companies have mines in production, but most of them are only a step above exploration companies. Those that do have mines usually have ones of a lower quality and need to open new ones to replace them when they run out of ore. However, when a new mine comes on line into production, earnings for these companies go through the roof.

Both the exploration and junior mining sectors are riddled with stock promoters and are high-risk speculations. There is a reason why penny stocks are worth only pennies. The difference between investing in a bar of bullion and investing in a penny stock is miles apart. There are no penny stocks in Fort Knox.

CHOOSING GOLD COMPANIES AS INVESTMENTS

When it comes to gold stocks, I invest in a core position of large producers through a gold mining stock ETF, such as GDX or GDXJ, which owns a swath of gold producers. Then, I build the rest of my gold stock portfolio around a basket of individual stocks in large and mid-tier producers or emerging producers. I believe they give me a good risk to reward ratio for each dollar I spend, since many of the shares of mid-tier companies double during rallies in the gold bull market. Most of them also trade over 1,000,000 shares a day. That is enough volume to allow me to build substantial positions and prevent any liquidity problems.

I look for mid-tier companies whose gold production is slated to increase over the next few years, enabling their earnings to grow exponentially even if the price of gold does not rise. They may be planning on reopening mines that have been out of production or have purchased mines from junior gold companies. These stocks often end up being the ones that go up the most in a bull market because of their high earnings growth. If you get into them early, you can even buy their earnings growth at a low valuation and make a bonanza.

In special cases, I invest in junior and exploration companies, but only after a full study of their projects. Most of these companies eventually either get bought out or go out of business. When you become one of their stockholders you become a shareholder and partner in their venture. You are making a bet not only that management can succeed, but that they are on your side and are interested in enhancing shareholder value by building a successful operation and aren't just trying to pad their pockets through stock jobbing. You need to know who the people are behind the company and understand their business model. Do they have properties worth exploring and developing, and will they have the resources to execute?

There are simple questions that you can ask. Whose money is already in the company? How much of the company's financing came from insiders and the management team and how much of it came from brokerage houses and individual investors? Is the management team paying itself in large salaries or do they expect to make money from gains in the share price along with their investors? If they are making stock transactions are they buying or selling shares?

What is the background of the management team? Have they built successful companies before? If they made mistakes in the past were they fooled themselves or did they fool their stockholders? Have the geologists involved in the company made successful discoveries in the past? What type of experience does the chief engineer have?

If you ask these simple questions than you'll invest your money with the top people in the industry. The other thing you need to know is how exploration and junior mining companies develop. This will help you evaluate whether or not an exploration company has a viable property or not and if a junior mining company is going to be able to develop a mine.

HOW MINING COMPANIES ARE DEVELOPED

Exploration is the first stage of development. Many exploration companies go to hot areas of the market where gold has already been discovered and mined. At some point in a gold bull market area plays develop and exploration companies appear out of nowhere to play off someone else's success. You need to be wary of a company whose only selling point is the area that it is in.

An exploration team will have its engineers survey its properties. Once they determine that there is likely a solid gold deposit, they will need to raise money in order to prove it. The company then drills holes on the property far apart from each other to get an idea of where the gold may be concentrated.

If the first drill results are successful, the company will carry out another drill test, called an "infill drilling" test. This test consists of drilling new holes in between the first ones in order to get a rough idea of the deposit size and ore grade. The drill results are then taken and the gold deposit is classified. You need to understand the classification system so that you can understand how viable the project is.

A deposit classified as a geological resource is the lowest grade deposit. Gold or silver has been found and a rough estimate has been made of its size and grade based on limited evidence. Further evaluation is needed. This classification is also called inferred, estimated, or drill-indicated. This level of resources has the lowest chance of ever being mined and it is best to stay away from exploration companies that tout such properties.

Most deposits are classified as a possible, probable, or proven reserve. Proven reserves have the highest confidence level and are measured with 50 foot drilling spacing. Probable reserves often use 100 foot drill spacing, while possible reserves use even wider drill spacing.

The Securities and Exchange Commission does not allow companies to include possible reserves when they total their ore reserves. Canada accepts them and allows mining companies to include them with their proven and possible reserves in press releases and shareholder reports. In reality, they are very low-grade properties and should not be counted as strong assets on a company's balance sheet. Be wary of Canadian mining companies whose portfolio is made up primarily of possible reserves.

If the exploration company's survey of a property is promising than it will go the next step, which is a feasibility study. This study further examines and defines the ore reserve and its size, identifies mining methods, estimates capital costs, and projects profitability and return on investment. A feasibility study can take up to three years to complete and once it is finished costs are calculated within a 15% margin. The process of going from exploration to a feasibility survey is what turns exploration companies into junior mining companies.

The next stage of development is the construction of the mine. This can cost a hundred million dollars, which is way more money than junior exploration companies have. If they can't finance the operation themselves than they will try to attract a larger partner to assist in the project or buy them out. If gold is in a bear trend than the project will sit idle until a new bull market in gold begins, a fact that causes many projects to sit in waiting.

The costs and time it takes to get the mine in operation can vary widely. A lot depends on the location of the property and the country that it is in. Stringent environmental laws and bureaucracy can drag out the process and raise costs. Once construction begins and the mine is operational more knowledge about the size and grade of the ore is obtained.

Even though a company that goes from exploration to production can be a bonanza for shareholders, it won't necessarily last. All mines run out of ore eventually and the company will have to find new gold reserves one day, if not at the current mine then at another property. If it doesn't than it will likely go bankrupt.

In the end, exploration and junior resource stocks can make profitable speculations, but they are almost all poor long-term investments. That is why, in the long-run gold, bullion acts as a better core investment position than a pile of penny stocks. Gold bullion is your Fort Knox.

CHAPTER IV
SOME OF MY TOP STOCK PICKS

I own many mining stocks. Some of them are core investment positions and some of them I trade in and out of. I write about the financial markets and give updates on what I see developing in precious metals and mining stocks on my website WallStreetWindow.com. I host a weekly podcast on Fridays about investing on this site. This is completely free and you can find it in Itunes by loading up Itunes and going to podcasts and then doing a search for "wallstreetwindow podcast."

I have written one top selling book titled, *Strategic Stock Trading*, in which I go through my Two Fold Formula for picking out stocks. If you have not read it yet you should order it and read it as a complimentary work to this book. I'd also suggest that you get my book, *The War State*, for a better understanding of the historical dimensions that have helped bring this moment in time for the precious metals markets. These books are available on Amazon.com.

I also run a small and private membership group of elite investors called Power Investor as a premium service on WallStreetWindow.com. One of the things I do in this group is look for one great stock or trading recommendation every week for the members. Most of the people in it are accredited investors and some are institutional investors.

These are serious people. All of us in this group are dedicated to helping each other profit as much as possible in the financial markets and we look out for new emerging bull markets. Out of respect for them, I cannot share with you all my mining stock picks in this book; however I can tell you about a few of them.

Here are three mining stocks that I consider my top picks for the next few years. Just so that you know, at time of publication of this book I own positions in all of them, even though I may sell them at anytime.

PICK NUMBER ONE:
PERSEUS MINING (TSX: PRU)

I have found the stocks that go up the most in a mining bull market are the stocks of the mining companies that have low valuations and high earnings growth. These companies start small and grow large by making capital investments in mines that are either going to increase production or begin production. The companies are going to simply produce and sell more ounces of gold or silver, which will translate into exponential earnings growth in the next few years.

But they do not only have high earnings growth, but a cheap valuation when you buy them too. That sets the stage for real investing with enormous upside potential.

For example, at the time of publication of this book Perseus Mining has a PEG ratio of 0.37. Let me tell you why this is important. The PEG ratio is a tool for you to use when picking stocks out. Most people look at either the price-to-earnings ratio, called simply the P/E ratio, or earnings growth estimates when they look to invest in a stock.

A P/E ratio divides the price of a stock by its annual earnings. So if a stock is trading at $10.00 a share and the company it represents makes $1.00 a share in earnings a year then it will have a P/E of 10. A P/E of 15 is typical in the stock market and in the real world when someone looks to buy a physical business they will look to buy something from five to seven times earnings. This means that it will take them five to seven years of earnings to pay the cost of purchase for the business.

In the stock market some people like to look for low P/E's to invest in as a way to find bargains. Other people though love to look for earnings growth stories instead. They like to find stocks of companies growing earnings by 20% or more a year.

These are hugely popular stocks with the general public, because they often generate big headlines and news reports of earnings growth. As the stock price goes up analysts tend to jump in and make predictions for even higher prices.

However, most people who invest in stocks like this pay no attention at all to the price they are paying when it comes to the stock. They simply buy earnings growth at any price. As a result they turn themselves into stock chasers that buy stocks simply because they have already gone up a lot and they hear good news about them. I do not consider such people to be serious investors, because they do not factor the valuation equation into their decision making, and often become bag holders when a bull cycle ends.

This is where the PEG ratio comes in. The PEG ratio looks at the estimated earnings growth for the next five years and divides the price by that figure. So it is tool that enables you to buy into high earnings growth stocks at a low valuation. A PEG ratio of one is considered to be fairly valued and a lower number is even better. I look for PEG ratios under 0.50. This means I invest in stocks that have both low valuations and high earnings growth. Perseus Mining fits the bill here.

Perseus Mining also has $0.08 of cash on hand and a book value of 0.85. It's trading at around forty cents cents a share, so it is at a fraction of its book value. The company has so much money in the bank that it does not need to do any financing anytime soon.

Perseus Mining, which is based in Australia, explores and develops mining gold properties in West Africa. Its principal projects include the Edikan Gold Mine that covers an area of approximately 650 square kilometers located in the Republic of Ghana; and the Sissingué Gold Project, that covers an area of 885 square kilometers located in the north of Côte d'Ivoire.

It currently produces gold at its Edikan Mine, but is spending money on structural improvements for it that will lower its mine production costs. It now costs $1,200 for it to mine an ounce of gold at this mine. The company expects to lower those costs to $1,050 by 2018 and increase production by 2015 to 240,000 ounces of gold a year. That's a lot of gold.

At the same time, it is exploring and drilling at its Sissingue Gold Project in order to decide if this property also should be developed into a functioning mining operation or not. It does have a mining plan to develop it, but hopes to revise this plan to the benefit of shareholders once it gets more exploration data for it in the next few months.

It also has a partnership with an unlisted junior mining company called West African Gold to explore properties right next to the red hot Hounde fault zone.

Perseus management has a track record of success. One member of its board of directors is Sean Harvey, who over ten years ago served as President and CEO of Orvana Minerals. It successfully explored and developed a property that was bought by Kinross and another property that was purchased by Wheaton River.

The CEO of Perseus Mining is Jeff Quartermaine. He has been in the business for 25 years. On March 27, 2014, he gave an interview to MidasLetter.com who asked him why is the stock so low.

Quartermine responded by saying, "Well, I think the reason is that the share price at which the company has been trading in recent times, has probably not reflected anywhere near the underlying value of the business. It's our view that the share price came down during the course of last year as a consequence of some macro factors around asset allocation in gold, things of that nature. And so the fall of the Perseus share price was quite pronounced."

"Now, at the same time as that was happening, we were making very material improvements in the operation at our major mine in Ghana, and improving productivity quite dramatically, so that we are in fact very well positioned to cope with a lower gold price environment, and very well positioned to move forward in the event that the gold price was to recover beyond the current level," Quartermine said.

The gold stock smash up of last year has created opportunities like Perseus mining to get in emerging junior mining stocks with high earnings growth and super low valuations. The way I see it is simple - Perseus is at a cheap valuation and is set to experience high earnings growth thanks to further development of its Edikan Gold Mine. This alone makes a tremendous leverage stock for higher gold prices. I consider the development projects Perseus has beyond Edikan as a simple juicy potential bonus play.

I can see it going over $1.00 a share and maybe even higher than that in a three to five year gold bull market.

PICK NUMBER TWO:
FREEPORT-MCMORAN COPPER AND GOLD
(NYSE: FCX)

Freeport-McMoRan Copper and Gold trades on the NYSE under the symbol FCX and, with a market cap over $37 billion, it is one of the largest mining companies in the world. Despite its size, though, FCX is poised for high earnings growth thanks to new mining projects that it plans to bring into production in the next few years. It has mining operations in Indonesia and Africa, and interests so large that it has recoverable proven and probable mineral reserves totaling 111.2 billion pounds of copper, 31.3 million ounces of gold, 3.26 billion pounds of molybdenum, 308.5 million ounces of silver and 0.87 billion pounds of cobalt, along with proven oil and gas reserves totaling 464 million barrels of oil equivalents.

FCX also produces natural gas and oil in North America, with operations mainly in California and the Gulf of Mexico. It is also developing the new and gigantic Haynesville Shale play in Louisiana.

It is the largest producer of molybdenum in the world and the largest publicly traded producer of copper. It's a mining and commodities giant. About 68% of its earnings come from metals mining and 32% from oil and natural gas.

It is set to increase its production of copper by 37% by 2015 thanks to billions of dollars worth of investments it has made in several mines around the world. This is translating into analyst estimates for over 20% annual earnings growth next year and 27% earnings growth per annum for the next five years.

FCX has a P/E of 11 when looking at next year's earnings, but thanks to these projected production increases and analyst estimates it is trading with a PEG ratio of 0.49. What this means is that FCX is a high growth earnings stock priced at a super low valuation in what is a beginning bull market sector.

Oh, and FCX pays an annual dividend of 3.60%. Put it all together and it is hard to find a better combination than all of this. If you do not have a position in mining stocks you may want to consider it a buy. If you are looking for something to buy and hold and get dividends from you may want to look at it really hard.

PICK NUMBER THREE: ATICO MINING (VANCOUVER: ATY)

Atico Mining is a small cap junior company with a market capitalization of around $75 million that trades on the Vancouver stock exchange under the symbol ATY. It is a small cap stock that posted high earnings growth potential with a super cheap valuation. The company owns the El Roble Mine in Colombia.

This property is the site of an operating underground copper and gold mine with nominal capacity of 400 tonnes per day. Off and on over the past 22 years the mine has processed 1.5 million tonnes of ore at an average grade of 2.5% copper and an estimated 2.5 g/t gold. Atico's underground drilling has discovered additional high-grade mineralization below level 2000, the deposit remains open at depth and strike. In plain english this means there is the potential for the discovery of a fantastic minable deposit.

Atico owns a 90% interest in the El Roble Mine and began to put it into production in the first quarter of this year. It has enough money in the bank from previous financings to put it into full production by the end of this year and they are on track to do it.

Analysts project that this accomplishment will earn Atico 5 cents a share in profit earnings this year and a full 15 cents a share in earnings in 2015. That means Atico is currently trading with a P/E of 5 when looking at next year's estimated earnings.

Atico management plans to do more drilling and exploration around the mine and has the potential to boost the value of this property, because it has already identified and mapped a 10 km stragraphic contact between basalt flows and pelagic sediments that control mineralization.

By the end of the year the profits from El Roble will enable Atico to become cash flow positive. The company management hopes to do more deals in the future to put more mining operations into production and become a mid-tier producer by purchasing more private mid-size mines or public small-scale mines with high exploration potential.

I have found in gold bull markets that the small cap stocks that go up the most are the ones that are about to increase production and are trading at a cheap valuation. The high earnings growth can cause a big increase in share prices.

The thing is, the analyst projections for the earnings growth in mining stocks such as Atico, and the others mentioned in this book, do not factor in higher gold prices. To show you what this means, consider this: the current industry average cost to mine an ounce of gold is $1,200. Gold prices at time of publication of this book are around $1300 an ounce. This means that while a $260 increase in gold prices means a 20% rise in gold prices, it means a 500%+ jump in earnings.

That is why these small cap stocks have the potential to go up so much in a gold bull market and demand our attention. They are essentially a leveraged investment to the price of gold that can create fortunes for people invested in the right ones.

Now these are just three stocks that I like and they may be at a much higher price point and valuation by the time you read this book. You may want to consult with a registered investment broker or adviser for another opinion if you are interested in them. You should not chase any stock higher and I may have even sold these stocks by the time you read this book. I constantly look for new stocks with good entry points at the WallStreetWindow website. You need to go there to see what is going on now in the markets and what I am doing.

ACKNOWLEDGEMENTS

Charts in this book courtesy of stockcharts.com. The government debt graphic used in chapter two is from the Government Accounting Office courtesy of Wikimedia Commons.

ABOUT THE AUTHOR

Michael Swanson received a Master's Degree in history from the University of Virginia and then dropped out of the college's Ph.D. program to enter the business world. He ran a hedge fund from 2003 until 2006 and runs the website wallstreetwindow.com.

Swanson is also the author of the history books *Danville, Virginia: and the Coming of the Modern South*, and *The War State: The Cold War Origins of the Military-Industrial Complex and the Power Elite, 1945-1963*, which is also available as an audio book. He is also the author of the investment book *Strategic Stock Trading*.

You can keep up with his thoughts on the financial markets and get more information on gold investing by going to his website wallstreetwindow.com and then joining his free email update list.

It is important to let as many people know about the developing gold trend as possible in order to help them. Word of mouth is critical for any author to succeed. If you enjoyed this book, please consider leaving a review at Amazon or your favorite book seller, even if it's only a line or two; it can make all of the difference and would be very much appreciated.

45797692R00050

Made in the USA
Charleston, SC
02 September 2015